'She kissed and kissed her with a hungry mouth.'

CHRISTINA ROSSETTI
Born 1830, London
Died 1894, London

ROSSETTI IN PENGUIN CLASSICS
The Complete Poems
The Penguin Book of Victorian Verse
The Pre-Raphaelites

PENGUIN CLASSICS

Published by the Penguin Group
Penguin Books Ltd, 80 Strand, London WC2R ORL, England
Penguin Group (USA) Inc., 375 Hudson Street, New York, New York 10014, USA
Penguin Group (Canada), 90 Eglinton Avenue East, Suite 700, Toronto, Ontario,
Canada M4P 2Y3 (a division of Pearson Penguin Canada Inc.)
Penguin Ireland, 25 St Stephen's Green, Dublin 2, Ireland
(a division of Penguin Books Ltd)
Penguin Group (Australia), 707 Collins Street, Melbourne, Victoria 3008, Australia
(a division of Pearson Australia Group Pty Ltd)
Penguin Books India Pvt Ltd, 11 Community Centre, Panchsheel Park,
New Delhi – 110 017, India
Penguin Group (NZ), 67 Apollo Drive, Rosedale, Auckland 0632, New Zealand
(a division of Pearson New Zealand Ltd)
Penguin Books (South Africa) (Pty) Ltd, Block D, Rosebank Office Park,
181 Jan Smuts Avenue, Parktown North, Gauteng 2193, South Africa

Penguin Books Ltd, Registered Offices: 80 Strand, London WC2R ORL, England

www.penguin.com

This selection published in Penguin Classics 2015
001

Set in 9/12.4 pt Baskerville 10 Pro
Typeset by Jouve (UK), Milton Keynes
Printed in Great Britain by Clays Ltd, St Ives plc

A CIP catalogue record for this book is available from the British Library

ISBN: 978-0-141-39766-5

www.greenpenguin.co.uk

Contents

Goblin Market

Morning and evening
Maids heard the goblins cry:
'Come buy our orchard fruits,
Come buy, come buy:
Apples and quinces,
Lemons and oranges,
Plump unpecked cherries,
Melons and raspberries,
Bloom-down-cheeked peaches,
Swart-headed mulberries,
Wild free-born cranberries,
Crab-apples, dewberries,
Pine-apples, blackberries,
Apricots, strawberries; –
All ripe together
In summer weather, –
Morns that pass by,
Fair eves that fly;
Come buy, come buy:
Our grapes fresh from the vine,
Pomegranates full and fine.
Dates and sharp bullaces,
Rare pears and greengages,
Damsons and bilberries,
Taste them and try:
Currants and gooseberries,
Bright-fire-like barberries,

Figs to fill your mouth,
Citrons from the South,
Sweet to tongue and sound to eye;
Come buy, come buy.'

  Evening by evening
Among the brookside rushes,
Laura bowed her head to hear,
Lizzie veiled her blushes:
Crouching close together
In the cooling weather,
With clasping arms and cautioning lips,
With tingling cheeks and finger tips.
'Lie close,' Laura said,
Pricking up her golden head:
'We must not look at goblin men,
We must not buy their fruits:
Who knows upon what soil they fed
Their hungry thirsty roots?'
'Come buy,' call the goblins
Hobbling down the glen.
'Oh,' cried Lizzie, 'Laura, Laura,
You should not peep at goblin men.'
Lizzie covered up her eyes,
Covered close lest they should look;
Laura reared her glossy head,
And whispered like the restless brook:
'Look, Lizzie, look, Lizzie,
Down the glen tramp little men.

One hauls a basket,
One bears a plate,
One lugs a golden dish
Of many pounds weight.
How fair the vine must grow
Whose grapes are so luscious;
How warm the wind must blow
Through those fruit bushes.'
'No,' said Lizzie: 'No, no, no;
Their offers should not charm us,
Their evil gifts would harm us.'
She thrust a dimpled finger
In each ear, shut eyes and ran:
Curious Laura chose to linger
Wondering at each merchant man.
One had a cat's face,
One whisked a tail,
One tramped at a rat's pace,
One crawled like a snail,
One like a wombat prowled obtuse and furry,
One like a ratel tumbled hurry skurry.
She heard a voice like voice of doves
Cooing all together:
They sounded kind and full of loves
In the pleasant weather.

Laura stretched her gleaming neck
Like a rush-imbedded swan,
Like a lily from the beck,

Like a moonlit poplar branch,
Like a vessel at the launch
When its last restraint is gone.

Backwards up the mossy glen
Turned and trooped the goblin men,
With their shrill repeated cry,
'Come buy, come buy.'
When they reached where Laura was
They stood stock still upon the moss,
Leering at each other,
Brother with queer brother;
Signalling each other,
Brother with sly brother.
One set his basket down,
One reared his plate;
One began to weave a crown
Of tendrils, leaves and rough nuts brown
(Men sell not such in any town);
One heaved the golden weight
Of dish and fruit to offer her:
'Come buy, come buy,' was still their cry.
Laura stared but did not stir,
Longed but had no money:
The whisk-tailed merchant bade her taste
In tones as smooth as honey,
The cat-faced purr'd,
The rat-paced spoke a word
Of welcome, and the snail-paced even was heard;

One parrot-voiced and jolly
Cried 'Pretty Goblin' still for 'Pretty Polly;' –
One whistled like a bird.

But sweet-tooth Laura spoke in haste:
'Good folk, I have no coin;
To take were to purloin:
I have no copper in my purse,
I have no silver either,
And all my gold is on the furze
That shakes in windy weather
Above the rusty heather.'
'You have much gold upon your head,'
They answered all together:
'Buy from us with a golden curl.'
She clipped a precious golden lock,
She dropped a tear more rare than pearl,
Then sucked their fruit globes fair or red:
Sweeter than honey from the rock,
Stronger than man-rejoicing wine,
Clearer than water flowed that juice;
She never tasted such before,
How should it cloy with length of use?
She sucked and sucked and sucked the more
Fruits which that unknown orchard bore;
She sucked until her lips were sore;
Then flung the emptied rinds away
But gathered up one kernel-stone,
And knew not was it night or day
As she turned home alone.

    Lizzie met her at the gate
Full of wise upbraidings:
'Dear, you should not stay so late,
Twilight is not good for maidens;
Should not loiter in the glen
In the haunts of goblin men.
Do you not remember Jeanie,
How she met them in the moonlight,
Took their gifts both choice and many,
Ate their fruits and wore their flowers
Plucked from bowers
Where summer ripens at all hours?
But ever in the noonlight
She pined and pined away;
Sought them by night and day,
Found them no more but dwindled and grew grey;
Then fell with the first snow,
While to this day no grass will grow
Where she lies low:
I planted daisies there a year ago
That never blow.
You should not loiter so.'
'Nay, hush,' said Laura:
'Nay, hush, my sister:
I ate and ate my fill,
Yet my mouth waters still;
To-morrow night I will
Buy more:' and kissed her:
'Have done with sorrow;
I'll bring you plums to-morrow

Fresh on their mother twigs,
Cherries worth getting;
You cannot think what figs
My teeth have met in,
What melons icy-cold
Piled on a dish of gold
Too huge for me to hold,
What peaches with a velvet nap,
Pellucid grapes without one seed:
Odorous indeed must be the mead
Whereon they grow, and pure the wave they drink
With lilies at the brink,
And sugar-sweet their sap.'

    Golden head by golden head,
Like two pigeons in one nest
Folded in each other's wings,
They lay down in their curtained bed:
Like two blossoms on one stem,
Like two flakes of new-fall'n snow,
Like two wands of ivory
Tipped with gold for awful kings.
Moon and stars gazed in at them,
Wind sang to them lullaby,
Lumbering owls forbore to fly,
Not a bat flapped to and fro
Round their rest:
Cheek to cheek and breast to breast
Locked together in one nest.

Early in the morning
When the first cock crowed his warning,
Neat like bees, as sweet and busy,
Laura rose with Lizzie:
Fetched in honey, milked the cows,
Aired and set to rights the house,
Kneaded cakes of whitest wheat,
Cakes for dainty mouths to eat,
Next churned butter, whipped up cream,
Fed their poultry, sat and sewed;
Talked as modest maidens should:
Lizzie with an open heart,
Laura in an absent dream,
One content, one sick in part;
One warbling for the mere bright day's delight,
One longing for the night.

At length slow evening came:
They went with pitchers to the reedy brook;
Lizzie most placid in her look,
Laura most like a leaping flame.
They drew the gurgling water from its deep;
Lizzie plucked purple and rich golden flags,
Then turning homewards said: 'The sunset flushes
Those furthest loftiest crags;
Come, Laura, not another maiden lags,
No wilful squirrel wags,
The beasts and birds are fast asleep.'

But Laura loitered still among the rushes
And said the bank was steep.

And said the hour was early still,
The dew not fall'n, the wind not chill:
Listening ever, but not catching
The customary cry,
'Come buy, come buy,'
With its iterated jingle
Of sugar-baited words:
Not for all her watching
Once discerning even one goblin
Racing, whisking, tumbling, hobbling;
Let alone the herds
That used to tramp along the glen,
In groups or single,
Of brisk fruit-merchant men.

Till Lizzie urged, 'O Laura, come;
I hear the fruit-call but I dare not look:
You should not loiter longer at this brook
Come with me home.
The stars rise, the moon bends her arc,
Each glowworm winks her spark,
Let us get home before the night grows dark:
For clouds may gather
Though this is summer weather,
Put out the lights and drench us through;
Then if we lost our way what should we do?'

Laura turned cold as stone
To find her sister heard that cry alone,
That goblin cry,
'Come buy our fruits, come buy.'
Must she then buy no more such dainty fruits?
Must she no more that succous pasture find,
Gone deaf and blind?
Her tree of life drooped from the root:
She said not one word in her heart's sore ache;
But peering thro' the dimness, nought discerning,
Trudged home, her pitcher dripping all the way;
So crept to bed, and lay
Silent till Lizzie slept;
Then sat up in a passionate yearning,
And gnashed her teeth for baulked desire, and wept
As if her heart would break.

Day after day, night after night,
Laura kept watch in vain
In sullen silence of exceeding pain.
She never caught again the goblin cry:
'Come buy, come buy;' –
She never spied the goblin men
Hawking their fruits along the glen:
But when the noon waxed bright
Her hair grew thin and grey;
She dwindled, as the fair full moon doth turn
To swift decay and burn
Her fire away.

One day remembering her kernel-stone
She set it by a wall that faced the south;
Dewed it with tears, hoped for a root,
Watched for a waxing shoot,
But there came none;
It never saw the sun,
It never felt the trickling moisture run:
While with sunk eyes and faded mouth
She dreamed of melons, as a traveller sees
False waves in desert drouth
With shade of leaf-crowned trees,
And burns the thirstier in the sandful breeze.

She no more swept the house,
Tended the fowls or cows,
Fetched honey, kneaded cakes of wheat,
Brought water from the brook:
But sat down listless in the chimney-nook
And would not eat.

Tender Lizzie could not bear
To watch her sister's cankerous care
Yet not to share.
She night and morning
Caught the goblins' cry:
'Come buy our orchard fruits,
Come buy, come buy:' –
Beside the brook, along the glen,
She heard the tramp of goblin men,
The voice and stir

Poor Laura could not hear;
Longed to buy fruit to comfort her,
But feared to pay too dear.
She thought of Jeanie in her grave,
Who should have been a bride;
But who for joys brides hope to have
Fell sick and died
In her gay prime,
In earliest Winter time,
With the first glazing rime,
With the first snow-fall of crisp Winter time.

Till Laura dwindling
Seemed knocking at Death's door:
Then Lizzie weighed no more
Better and worse;
But put a silver penny in her purse,
Kissed Laura, crossed the heath with clumps of furze
At twilight, halted by the brook:
And for the first time in her life
Began to listen and look.

Laughed every goblin
When they spied her peeping:
Came towards her hobbling,
Flying, running, leaping,
Puffing and blowing,
Chuckling, clapping, crowing,
Clucking and gobbling,
Mopping and mowing,
Full of airs and graces,

Pulling wry faces,
Demure grimaces,
Cat-like and rat-like,
Ratel- and wombat-like,
Snail-paced in a hurry,
Parrot-voiced and whistler,
Helter skelter, hurry skurry,
Chattering like magpies,
Fluttering like pigeons,
Gliding like fishes, –
Hugged her and kissed her,
Squeezed and caressed her:
Stretched up their dishes,
Panniers, and plates:
'Look at our apples
Russet and dun,
Bob at our cherries,
Bite at our peaches,
Citrons and dates,
Grapes for the asking,
Pears red with basking
Out in the sun,
Plums on their twigs;
Pluck them and suck them.
Pomegranates, figs.' –

'Good folk,' said Lizzie,
Mindful of Jeanie:
'Give me much and many;' –
Held out her apron,

Tossed them her penny.
'Nay, take a seat with us,
Honour and eat with us,'
They answered grinning:
'Our feast is but beginning.
Night yet is early,
Warm and dew-pearly,
Wakeful and starry:
Such fruits as these
No man can carry;
Half their bloom would fly,
Half their dew would dry,
Half their flavour would pass by.
Sit down and feast with us,
Be welcome guest with us,
Cheer you and rest with us.' –
'Thank you,' said Lizzie: 'But one waits
At home alone for me:
So without further parleying,
If you will not sell me any
Of your fruits though much and many,
Give me back my silver penny
I tossed you for a fee.' –
They began to scratch their pates,
No longer wagging, purring,
But visibly demurring,
Grunting and snarling.
One called her proud,
Cross-grained, uncivil;
Their tones waxed loud,

Their looks were evil.
Lashing their tails
They trod and hustled her,
Elbowed and jostled her,
Clawed with their nails,
Barking, mewing, hissing, mocking,
Tore her gown and soiled her stocking,
Twitched her hair out by the roots,
Stamped upon her tender feet,
Held her hands and squeezed their fruits
Against her mouth to make her eat.

White and golden Lizzie stood,
Like a lily in a flood, –
Like a rock of blue-veined stone
Lashed by tides obstreperously, –
Like a beacon left alone
In a hoary roaring sea,
Sending up a golden fire, –
Like a fruit-crowned orange-tree
White with blossoms honey-sweet
Sore beset by wasp and bee, –
Like a royal virgin town
Topped with gilded dome and spire
Close beleaguered by a fleet
Mad to tug her standard down.

One may lead a horse to water,
Twenty cannot make him drink.
Though the goblins cuffed and caught her,
Coaxed and fought her,

Bullied and besought her,
Scratched her, pinched her black as ink,
Kicked and knocked her,
Mauled and mocked her,
Lizzie uttered not a word;
Would not open lip from lip
Lest they should cram a mouthful in:
But laughed in heart to feel the drip
Of juice that syrupped all her face,
And lodged in dimples of her chin,
And streaked her neck which quaked like curd.
At last the evil people
Worn out by her resistance
Flung back her penny, kicked their fruit
Along whichever road they took,
Not leaving root or stone or shoot;
Some writhed into the ground,
Some dived into the brook
With ring and ripple,
Some scudded on the gale without a sound,
Some vanished in the distance.

    In a smart, ache, tingle,
Lizzie went her way;
Knew not was it night or day;
Sprang up the bank, tore thro' the furze,
Threaded copse and dingle,
And heard her penny jingle
Bouncing in her purse, –
Its bounce was music to her ear.

She ran and ran
As if she feared some goblin man
Dogged her with gibe or curse
Or something worse:
But not one goblin skurried after,
Nor was she pricked by fear;
The kind heart made her windy-paced
That urged her home quite out of breath with haste
And inward laughter.

   She cried 'Laura,' up the garden,
'Did you miss me?
Come and kiss me.
Never mind my bruises,
Hug me, kiss me, suck my juices
Squeezed from goblin fruits for you,
Goblin pulp and goblin dew.
Eat me, drink me, love me;
Laura, make much of me:
For your sake I have braved the glen
And had to do with goblin merchant men.'

    Laura started from her chair,
Flung her arms up in the air,
Clutched her hair:
'Lizzie, Lizzie, have you tasted
For my sake the fruit forbidden?
Must your light like mine be hidden,
Your young life like mine be wasted,
Undone in mine undoing
And ruined in my ruin,

Thirsty, cankered, goblin-ridden?' –
She clung about her sister,
Kissed and kissed and kissed her:
Tears once again
Refreshed her shrunken eyes,
Dropping like rain
After long sultry drouth;
Shaking with aguish fear, and pain,
She kissed and kissed her with a hungry mouth.

Her lips began to scorch,
That juice was wormwood to her tongue,
She loathed the feast:
Writhing as one possessed she leaped and sung,
Rent all her robe, and wrung
Her hands in lamentable haste,
And beat her breast.
Her locks streamed like the torch
Borne by a racer at full speed,
Or like the mane of horses in their flight,
Or like an eagle when she stems the light
Straight toward the sun,
Or like a caged thing freed,
Or like a flying flag when armies run.

Swift fire spread through her veins, knocked at her
heart,
Met the fire smouldering there
And overbore its lesser flame;
She gorged on bitterness without a name:
Ah! fool, to choose such part

Of soul-consuming care!
Sense failed in the mortal strife:
Like the watch-tower of a town
Which an earthquake shatters down,
Like a lightning-stricken mast,
Like a wind-uprooted tree
Spun about,
Like a foam-topped waterspout
Cast down headlong in the sea,
She fell at last;
Pleasure past and anguish past,
Is it death or is it life?

    Life out of death.
That night long Lizzie watched by her,
Counted her pulse's flagging stir,
Felt for her breath,
Held water to her lips, and cooled her face
With tears and fanning leaves:
But when the first birds chirped about their eaves,
And early reapers plodded to the place
Of golden sheaves,
And dew-wet grass
Bowed in the morning winds so brisk to pass,
And new buds with new day
Opened of cup-like lilies on the stream,
Laura awoke as from a dream,
Laughed in the innocent old way,
Hugged Lizzie but not twice or thrice;
Her gleaming locks showed not one thread of grey,

Her breath was sweet as May
And light danced in her eyes.

Days, weeks, months, years,
Afterwards, when both were wives
With children of their own;
Their mother-hearts beset with fears,
Their lives bound up in tender lives;
Laura would call the little ones
And tell them of her early prime,
Those pleasant days long gone
Of not-returning time:
Would talk about the haunted glen,
The wicked, quaint fruit-merchant men,
Their fruits like honey to the throat
But poison in the blood;
(Men sell not such in any town:)
Would tell them how her sister stood
In deadly peril to do her good,
And win the fiery antidote:
Then joining hands to little hands
Would bid them cling together,
'For there is no friend like a sister
In calm or stormy weather;
To cheer one on the tedious way,
To fetch one if one goes astray,
To lift one if one totters down,
To strengthen whilst one stands.'

Dream Land

Where sunless rivers weep
Their waves into the deep,
She sleeps a charmèd sleep:
    Awake her not.
Led by a single star,
She came from very far
To seek where shadows are
    Her pleasant lot.

She left the rosy morn,
She left the fields of corn,
For twilight cold and lorn
    And water springs.
Through sleep, as through a veil,
She sees the sky look pale,
And hears the nightingale
    That sadly sings.

Rest, rest, a perfect rest
Shed over brow and breast;
Her face is toward the west,
    The purple land.
She cannot see the grain
Ripening on hill and plain;
She cannot feel the rain
    Upon her hand.

Christina Rossetti

Rest, rest, for evermore
Upon a mossy shore;
Rest, rest at the heart's core
    Till time shall cease:
Sleep that no pain shall wake,
Night that no morn shall break
Till joy shall overtake
    Her perfect peace.

Song

When I am dead, my dearest,
    Sing no sad songs for me;
Plant thou no roses at my head,
    Nor shady cypress tree:
Be the green grass above me
    With showers and dewdrops wet:
And if thou wilt, remember,
    And if thou wilt, forget.

I shall not see the shadows,
    I shall not feel the rain;
I shall not hear the nightingale
    Sing on as if in pain:
And dreaming through the twilight
    That doth not rise nor set,
Haply I may remember,
    And haply may forget.

An End

Love, strong as Death, is dead
Come, let us make his bed
Among the dying flowers:
A green turf at his head;
And a stone at his feet,
Whereon we may sit
In the quiet evening hours.

He was born in the Spring,
And died before the harvesting:
On the last warm summer day
He left us; he would not stay
For Autumn twilight cold and grey.
Sit we by his grave, and sing
He is gone away.

To few chords and sad and low
Sing we so:
Be our eyes fixed on the grass
Shadow-veiled as the years pass,
While we think of all that was
In the long ago.

A Pause of Thought

I looked for that which is not, nor can be,
    And hope deferred made my heart sick in truth:
    But years must pass before a hope of youth
      Is resigned utterly.

I watched and waited with a steadfast will:
    And though the object seemed to flee away
    That I so longed for, ever day by day
      I watched and waited still.

Sometimes I said: This thing shall be no more;
    My expectation wearies and shall cease;
    I will resign it now and be at peace:
      Yet never gave it o'er.

Sometimes I said: It is an empty name
    I long for; to a name why should I give
    The peace of all the days I have to live? –
      Yet gave it all the same.

Alas, thou foolish one! alike unfit
    For healthy joy and salutary pain:
    Thou knowest the chase useless, and again
      Turnest to follow it.

Sweet Death

The sweetest blossoms die.
    And so it was that, going day by day
    Unto the Church to praise and pray,
And crossing the green churchyard thoughtfully,
    I saw how on the graves the flowers
    Shed their fresh leaves in showers,
And how their perfume rose up to the sky
    Before it passed away.

The youngest blossoms die.
    They die and fall and nourish the rich earth
    From which they lately had their birth;
Sweet life, but sweeter death that passeth by
    And is as though it had not been: –
    All colours turn to green;
The bright hues vanish and the odours fly,
    The grass hath lasting worth.

And youth and beauty die.
    So be it, O my God, Thou God of truth:
    Better than beauty and than youth
Are Saints and Angels, a glad company;
    And Thou, O Lord, our Rest and Ease,
    Art better far than these.
Why should we shrink from our full harvest? why
    Prefer to glean with Ruth?

A Birthday

My heart is like a singing bird
    Whose nest is in a watered shoot;
My heart is like an appletree
    Whose boughs are bent with thickset fruit;
My heart is like a rainbow shell
    That paddles in a halcyon sea;
My heart is gladder than all these
    Because my love is come to me.

Raise me a dais of silk and down;
    Hang it with vair and purple dyes;
Carve it in doves, and pomegranates,
    And peacocks with a hundred eyes;
Work it in gold and silver grapes,
    In leaves, and silver fleurs-de-lys;
Because the birthday of my life
    Is come, my love is come to me.

Babylon the Great

Foul is she and ill-favoured, set askew:
　　Gaze not upon her till thou dream her fair,
　　Lest she should mesh thee in her wanton hair,
Adept in arts grown old yet ever new.
Her heart lusts not for love, but thro' and thro'
　　For blood, as spotted panther lusts in lair;
　　No wine is in her cup, but filth is there
Unutterable, with plagues hid out of view.
Gaze not upon her; for her dancing whirl
　　Turns giddy the fixed gazer presently:
　　Gaze not upon her, lest thou be as she
　　　When at the far end of her long desire
Her scarlet vest and gold and gem and pearl
　　And she amid her pomp are set on fire.

On Keats

A garden in a garden: a green spot
    Where all is green: most fitting slumber-place
    For the strong man grown weary of a race
Soon over. Unto him a goodly lot
Hath fallen in fertile ground; there thorns are not,
    But his own daisies; silence, full of grace,
    Surely hath shed a quiet on his face;
His earth is but sweet leaves that fall and rot.
What was his record of himself, ere he
    Went from us? 'Here lies one whose name was writ
    In water.' While the chilly shadows flit
    Of sweet St Agnes' Eve, while basil springs –
    His name, in every humble heart that sings,
Shall be a fountain of love, verily.

In an Artist's Studio

One face looks out from all his canvases,
    One selfsame figure sits or walks or leans:
    We found her hidden just behind those screens,
That mirror gave back all her loveliness.
A queen in opal or in ruby dress,
    A nameless girl in freshest summer-greens,
    A saint, an angel – every canvas means
The same one meaning, neither more nor less.
He feeds upon her face by day and night,
    And she with true kind eyes looks back on him,
Fair as the moon and joyful as the light:
    Not wan with waiting, not with sorrow dim;
Not as she is, but was when hope shone bright;
    Not as she is, but as she fills his dream.

The Queen of Hearts

How comes it, Flora, that, whenever we
Play cards together, you invariably,
> However the pack parts,
> Still hold the Queen of Hearts?

I've scanned you with a scrutinizing gaze,
Resolved to fathom these your secret ways:
> But, sift them as I will,
> Your ways are secret still.

I cut and shuffle; shuffle, cut, again;
But all my cutting, shuffling, proves in vain:
> Vain hope, vain forethought too;
> That Queen still falls to you.

I dropped her once, prepense; but, ere the deal
Was dealt, your instinct seemed her loss to feel:
> 'There should be one card more,'
> You said, and searched the floor.

I cheated once; I made a private notch
In Heart-Queen's back, and kept a lynx-eyed watch;
> Yet such another back
> Deceived me in the pack;

The Queen of Clubs assumed by arts unknown
An imitative dint that seemed my own;
> This notch, not of my doing,
> Misled me to my ruin.

It baffles me to puzzle out the clue,
Which must be skill, or craft, or luck in you:
Unless, indeed, it be
Natural affinity.

A Christmas Carol

In the bleak mid-winter
    Frosty wind made moan,
Earth stood hard as iron,
    Water like a stone;
Snow had fallen, snow on snow,
    Snow on snow,
In the bleak mid-winter
    Long ago.

Our God, Heaven cannot hold Him
    Nor earth sustain;
Heaven and earth shall flee away
    When He comes to reign:
In the bleak mid-winter
    A stable-place sufficed
The Lord God Almighty
    Jesus Christ.

Enough for Him, whom cherubim
    Worship night and day,
A breastful of milk
    And a mangerful of hay;
Enough for Him, whom angels,
    Fall down before,
The ox and ass and camel
    Which adore.

Angels and archangels
    May have gathered there,
Cherubim and seraphim
    Throng'd the air,
But only His mother
    In her maiden bliss
Worshipped the Beloved
    With a kiss.

What can I give Him,
    Poor as I am?
If I were a shepherd
    I would bring a lamb,
If I were a Wise Man
    I would do my part, –
Yet what I can I give Him,
    Give my heart.

An Old-World Thicket

'Una selva oscura.'

– Dante

Awake or sleeping (for I know not which)
    I was or was not mazed within a wood
    Where every mother-bird brought up her brood
      Safe in some leafy niche
Of oak or ash, of cypress or of beech,

Of silvery aspen trembling delicately,
    Of plane or warmer-tinted sycomore,
    Of elm that dies in secret from the core,
      Of ivy weak and free,
Of pines, of all green lofty things that be.

Such birds they seemed as challenged each desire;
    Like spots of azure heaven upon the wing,
    Like downy emeralds that alight and sing,
      Like actual coals on fire,
Like anything they seemed, and everything.

Such mirth they made, such warblings and such chat
    With tongue of music in a well-tuned beak,
    They seemed to speak more wisdom than we speak,
      To make our music flat
And all our subtlest reasonings wild or weak.

Their meat was nought but flowers like butterflies,
    With berries coral-coloured or like gold;
        Their drink was only dew, which blossoms hold
            Deep where the honey lies;
Their wings and tails were lit by sparkling eyes.

The shade wherein they revelled was a shade
    That danced and twinkled to the unseen sun;
        Branches and leaves cast shadows one by one,
            And all their shadows swayed
In breaths of air that rustled and that played.

A sound of waters neither rose nor sank,
    And spread a sense of freshness through the air;
        It seemed not here or there, but everywhere,
            As if the whole earth drank,
Root fathom-deep and strawberry on its bank.

But I who saw such things as I have said
    Was overdone with utter weariness;
        And walked in care, as one whom fears oppress
            Because above his head
Death hangs, or damage, or the dearth of bread.

Each sore defeat of my defeated life
    Faced and outfaced me in that bitter hour;
        And turned to yearning palsy all my power,
            And all my peace to strife,
Self stabbing self with keen lack-pity knife.

Sweetness of beauty moved me to despair,
    Stung me to anger by its mere content,

Made me all lonely on that way I went,
　　Piled care upon my care,
Brimmed full my cup, and stripped me empty and bare:

For all that was but showed what all was not,
　　But gave clear proof of what might never be;
　　Making more destitute my poverty,
　　　And yet more blank my lot,
And me much sadder by its jubilee.

Therefore I sat me down: for wherefore walk?
　　And closed mine eyes: for wherefore see or hear?
　　Alas, I had no shutter to mine ear,
　　　And could not shun the talk
Of all rejoicing creatures far or near.

Without my will I hearkened and I heard
　　(Asleep or waking, for I know not which),
　　Till note by note the music changed its pitch;
　　　Bird ceased to answer bird,
And every wind sighed softly if it stirred.

The drip of widening waters seemed to weep,
　　All fountains sobbed and gurgled as they sprang,
　　Somewhere a cataract cried out in its leap
　　　Sheer down a headlong steep;
High over all cloud-thunders gave a clang.

Such universal sound of lamentation
　　I heard and felt, fain not to feel or hear;
　　Nought else there seemed but anguish far and near;
　　　Nought else but all creation
Moaning and groaning wrung by pain or fear,

Shuddering in the misery of its doom:
> My heart then rose a rebel against light,
>> Scouring all earth and heaven and depth and height,
>>> Ingathering wrath and gloom,
Ingathering wrath to wrath and night to night.

Ah me, the bitterness of such revolt,
> All impotent, all hateful, and all hate,
>> That kicks and breaks itself against the bolt
>>> Of an imprisoning fate,
And vainly shakes, and cannot shake the gate.

Agony to agony, deep called to deep,
> Out of the deep I called of my desire;
>> My strength was weakness and my heart was fire;
>>> Mine eyes that would not weep
Or sleep, scaled height and depth, and could not sleep;

The eyes, I mean, of my rebellious soul,
> For still my bodily eyes were closed and dark:
>> A random thing I seemed without a mark,
>>> Racing without a goal,
Adrift upon life's sea without an ark.

More leaden than the actual self of lead
> Outer and inner darkness weighed on me.
>> The tide of anger ebbed. Then fierce and free
>>> Surged full above my head
The moaning tide of helpless misery.

Why should I breathe, whose breath was but a sigh?
    Why should I live, who drew such painful breath?
    Oh weary work, the unanswerable why! –
        Yet I, why should I die,
Who had no hope in life, no hope in death?

Grasses and mosses and the fallen leaf
    Make peaceful bed for an indefinite term;
    But underneath the grass there gnaws a worm –
        Haply, there gnaws a grief –
Both, haply always; not, as now, so brief.

The pleasure I remember, it is past;
    The pain I feel, is passing passing by;
    Thus all the world is passing, and thus I:
        All things that cannot last
Have grown familiar, and are born to die.

And being familiar, have so long been borne
    That habit trains us not to break but bend:
    Mourning grows natural to us who mourn
        In foresight of an end,
But that which ends not who shall brave or mend?

Surely the ripe fruits tremble on their bough,
    They cling and linger trembling till they drop:
    I, trembling, cling to dying life; for how
        Face the perpetual Now?
Birthless and deathless, void of start or stop,

Void of repentance, void of hope and fear,
    Of possibility, alternative,
     Of all that ever made us bear to live
      From night to morning here,
Of promise even which has no gift to give.

The wood, and every creature of the wood,
    Seemed mourning with me in an undertone;
     Soft scattered chirpings and a windy moan,
      Trees rustling where they stood
And shivered, showed compassion for my mood.

Rage to despair; and now despair had turned
    Back to self-pity and mere weariness,
     With yearnings like a smouldering fire that burned,
      And might grow more or less,
And might die out or wax to white excess.

Without, within me, music seemed to be;
    Something not music, yet most musical,
     Silence and sound in heavenly harmony;
      At length a pattering fall
Of feet, a bell, and bleatings, broke through all.

Then I looked up. The wood lay in a glow
    From golden sunset and from ruddy sky;
     The sun had stooped to earth though once so high;
      Had stooped to earth, in slow
Warm dying loveliness brought near and low.

Each water drop made answer to the light,
    Lit up a spark and showed the sun his face;

Soft purple shadows paved the grassy space
    And crept from height to height,
From height to loftier height crept up apace.

While opposite the sun a gazing moon
    Put on his glory for her coronet,
    Kindling her luminous coldness to its noon,
      As his great splendour set;
One only star made up her train as yet.

Each twig was tipped with gold, each leaf was edged
    And veined with gold from the gold-flooded west;
    Each mother-bird, and mate-bird, and unfledged
      Nestling, and curious nest,
    Displayed a gilded moss or beak or breast.

And filing peacefully between the trees,
    Having the moon behind them, and the sun
    Full in their meek mild faces, walked at ease
      A homeward flock, at peace
With one another and with every one.

A patriarchal ram with tinkling bell
    Led all his kin; sometimes one browsing sheep
    Hung back a moment, or one lamb would leap
      And frolic in a dell;
Yet still they kept together, journeying well,

And bleating, one or other, many or few,
    Journeying together toward the sunlit west;
    Mild face by face, and woolly breast by breast,
      Patient, sun-brightened too,
Still journeying toward the sunset and their rest.

Spring Quiet

Gone were but the Winter,
    Come were but the Spring,
I would go to a covert
    Where the birds sing;

Where in the whitethorn
    Singeth a thrush,
And a robin sings
    In the holly-bush.

Full of fresh scents
    Are the budding boughs
Arching high over
    A cool green house:

Full of sweet scents,
    And whispering air
Which sayeth softly:
    'We spread no snare;

'Here dwell in safety,
    Here dwell alone,
With a clear stream
    And a mossy stone.

'Here the sun shineth
    Most shadily;
Here is heard an echo
    Of the far sea,
    Though far off it be.'

Up-Hill

Does the road wind up-hill all the way?
    Yes, to the very end.
Will the day's journey take the whole long day?
    From morn to night, my friend.

But is there for the night a resting-place?
    A roof for when the slow dark hours begin.
May not the darkness hide it from my face?
    You cannot miss that inn.

Shall I meet other wayfarers at night?
    Those who have gone before.
Then must I knock, or call when just in sight?
    They will not keep you standing at that door.

Shall I find comfort, travel-sore and weak?
    Of labour you shall find the sum.
Will there be beds for me and all who seek?
    Yea, beds for all who come.

Song

Two doves upon the selfsame branch,
    Two lilies on a single stem,
Two butterflies upon one flower: –
    Oh happy they who look on them!

Who look upon them hand in hand
    Flushed in the rosy summer light;
Who look upon them hand in hand,
    And never give a thought to night.

A Dirge

Why were you born when the snow was falling?
You should have come to the cuckoo's calling,
Or when grapes are green in the cluster,
Or at least when lithe swallows muster
    For their far off flying
    From summer dying.

Why did you die when the lambs were cropping?
You should have died at the apples' dropping,
When the grasshopper comes to trouble,
And the wheat-fields are sodden stubble,
    And all winds go sighing
    For sweet things dying.

A Frog's Fate

Contemptuous of his home beyond
The village and the village pond,
A large-souled Frog who spurned each byeway
Hopped along the imperial highway.

Nor grunting pig nor barking dog
Could disconcert so great a Frog.
The morning dew was lingering yet,
His sides to cool, his tongue to wet:
The night-dew when the night should come
A travelled Frog would send him home.

Not so, alas! The wayside grass
Sees him no more: not so, alas!
A broad-wheeled waggon unawares
Ran him down, his joys, his cares.
From dying choke one feeble croak

The Frog's perpetual silence broke: –
'Ye buoyant Frogs, ye great and small,
Even I am mortal after all!
My road to fame turns out a wry way:
I perish on the hideous highway;
Oh for my old familiar byeway!'

The choking Frog sobbed and was gone;
The Waggoner strode whistling on.
Unconscious of the carnage done,
Whistling that Waggoner strode on –

Whistling (it may have happened so)
'A froggy would a-wooing go.'
A hypothetic frog trolled he
Obtuse to a reality.

O rich and poor, O great and small,
Such oversights beset us all:
The mangled Frog abides incog,
The uninteresting actual frog:
The hypothetic frog alone
Is the one frog we dwell upon.

My Dream

Hear now a curious dream I dreamed last night,
Each word whereof is weighed and sifted truth.

I stood beside Euphrates while it swelled
Like overflowing Jordan in its youth:
It waxed and coloured sensibly to sight;
Till out of myriad pregnant waves there welled
Young crocodiles, a gaunt blunt-featured crew,
Fresh-hatched perhaps and daubed with birthday dew.
The rest if I should tell, I fear my friend
My closest friend would deem the facts untrue;
And therefore it were wisely left untold;
Yet if you will, why hear it to the end.

Each crocodile was girt with massive gold
And polished stones that with their wearers grew:
But one there was who waxed beyond the rest,
Wore kinglier girdle and a kingly crown,
Whilst crowns and orbs and sceptres starred his breast.
All gleamed compact and green with scale on scale,
But special burnishment adorned his mail
And special terror weighed upon his frown;
His punier brethren quaked before his tail,
Broad as a rafter, potent as a flail.
So he grew lord and master of his kin:
But who shall tell the tale of all their woes?
An execrable appetite arose,
He battened on them, crunched, and sucked them in.

He knew no law, he feared no binding law,
But ground them with inexorable jaw:
The luscious fat distilled upon his chin,
Exuded from his nostrils and his eyes,
While still like hungry death he fed his maw;
Till every minor crocodile being dead
And buried too, himself gorged to the full,
He slept with breath oppressed and unstrung claw.
Oh marvel passing strange which next I saw:
In sleep he dwindled to the common size,
And all the empire faded from his coat.
Then from far off a wingèd vessel came,
Swift as a swallow, subtle as a flame:
I know not what it bore of freight or host,
But white it was as an avenging ghost.
It levelled strong Euphrates in its course;
Supreme yet weightless as an idle mote
It seemed to tame the waters without force
Till not a murmur swelled or billow beat:
Lo, as the purple shadow swept the sands,
The prudent crocodile rose on his feet
And shed appropriate tears and wrung his hands.

What can it mean? you ask. I answer not
For meaning, but myself must echo, What?
And tell it as I saw it on the spot.

Nursery Rhymes from Sing-Song

My baby has a father and a mother,
    Rich little baby!
Fatherless, motherless, I know another
    Forlorn as may be:
    Poor little baby!

Our little baby fell asleep,
    And may not wake again
For days and days, and weeks and weeks;
    But then he'll wake again,
And come with his own pretty look,
    And kiss Mamma again.

    Baby cry—
    Oh fie!—
At the physic in the cup:
    Gulp it twice
    And gulp it thrice,
Baby gulp it up.

Eight o'clock;
The postman's knock!
Five letters for Papa;
    One for Lou,
    And none for you,
And three for dear Mamma.

Bread and milk for breakfast,
   And woollen frocks to wear,
And a crumb for robin redbreast
   On the cold days of the year.

There's snow on the fields,
   And cold in the cottage,
While I sit in the chimney nook
   Supping hot pottage.

My clothes are soft and warm,
   Fold upon fold,
But I'm so sorry for the poor
   Out in the cold.

Dead in the cold, a song-singing thrush,
Dead at the foot of a snowberry bush,—
Weave him a coffin of rush,
Dig him a grave where the soft mosses grow,
Raise him a tombstone of snow.

I dug and dug amongst the snow,
And thought the flowers would never grow;
I dug and dug amongst the sand,
And still no green thing came to hand.

Melt, O snow! the warm winds blow
To thaw the flowers and melt the snow;
But all the winds from every land
Will rear no blossom from the sand.

A city plum is not a plum;
A dumb-bell is no bell, though dumb;
A party rat is not a rat;
A sailor's cat is not a cat;
A soldier's frog is not a frog;
A captain's log is not a log.

Your brother has a falcon,
    Your sister has a flower;
But what is left for mannikin,
    Born within an hour?

I'll nurse you on my knee, my knee,
    My own little son;
I'll rock you, rock you, in my arms,
    My least little one.

Hear what the mournful linnets say:
    'We built our nest compact and warm,
But cruel boys came round our way
    And took our summerhouse by storm.

'They crushed the eggs so neatly laid;
    So now we sit with drooping wing,
And watch the ruin they have made,
    Too late to build, too sad to sing.'

A baby's cradle with no baby in it,
    A baby's grave where autumn leaves drop sere;
The sweet soul gathered home to Paradise,
    The body waiting here.

Hope is like a harebell trembling from its birth,
Love is like a rose the joy of all the earth;
Faith is like a lily lifted high and white,
Love is like a lovely rose the world's delight;
Harebells and sweet lilies show a thornless growth,
But the rose with all its thorns excels them both.

O wind, why do you never rest,
    Wandering, whistling to and fro,
Bringing rain out of the west,
    From the dim north bringing snow?

A linnet in a gilded cage,—
    A linnet on a bough,—
In frosty winter one might doubt
    Which bird is luckier now.

But let the trees burst out in leaf,
    And nests be on the bough,
Which linnet is the luckier bird,
    Oh who could doubt it now?

Wrens and robins in the hedge,
    Wrens and robins here and there;
Building, perching, pecking, fluttering,
      Everywhere!

My baby has a mottled fist,
    My baby has a neck in creases;
My baby kisses and is kissed,
    For he's the very thing for kisses.

Why did baby die,
Making Father sigh,
Mother cry?

Flowers, that bloom to die,
Make no reply
Of 'why?'
But bow and die.

If all were rain and never sun,
    No bow could span the hill;
If all were sun and never rain,
    There'd be no rainbow still.

O wind, where have you been,
    That you blow so sweet?
Among the violets
    Which blossom at your feet.
The honeysuckle waits
    For Summer and for heat.
But violets in the chilly Spring
    Make the turf so sweet.

Heartsease in my garden bed,
    With sweetwilliam white and red,
Honeysuckle on my wall:—
    Heartsease blossoms in my heart
When sweet William comes to call,
    But it withers when we part,
And the honey-trumpets fall.

If I were a Queen,
    What would I do?
I'd make you King,
    And I'd wait on you.

If I were a King,
    What would I do?
I'd make you Queen,
    For I'd marry you.